UNDER FORESTS
OF FUTILITY

UNDER FORESTS OF FUTILITY

Rasu-Yong Tugen,

Baroness de Tristeombre

gnOme

ISBN-13: 978-0692174197 (gnOme books)
ISBN-10: 0692174192

Address inquiries to: gnOmebooks@gmail.com

Wenn ich beim Waldesrauschen hier
Gedankenvoll gesessen...

~ Joseph von Eichendorff, Gedichte (1837)

Mottled microscopic blackened green,
scraped across shadowed geometries.
Lyricism. Withering. Dark augur of
tendril-like melodies in the delirious sky.

Outside the glaring twilight
— crawling hushed whispers
spurt forth half-dead worms.

Conspiracy of uncultivated
winds, glimmering below
sullen, stellar treetops.

Thoughts as bewildered
as tangled black hair.
Starlings fall into the sky
from vespers of green
decay.

A single moon lights ten thousand subterranean forests. Pools of black graphite and dirtied silver freeze into the blind night corridors of the deathless sky. Ink-stained lichens gently envelop the black gravity of our tired and withering flesh.

Under cathedral skies of
tectonic ice — horizonless
erosion illuminated by the
faintest of apprehensions.
The dust of bone become
green stars.

Each hour our trembling
frames sink lower, drifting
quietly down the starless
corridors of obsidian night.

The disquieting, sleepwalking
stillness of late afternoon skies.
Night of sorrowful countenance.
Swaying trees.

Twilight sighs of cedars
and pine — damp moss
covers the four walls of
suspicion, gently reaching
across my jewel-crusted
skull.

We adhere to the form of
sacred sleeping forest
geometries. Fear. Weeping.
Billows of purple amethyst
beneath your chest and
abdomen.

The planet a grave mound. All the ages reduced to one. Sullenly we count all directions in a single darkness. When you're born, you cry. When you die, others cry.

At night, screech-owls
silently drip from roots
of sallow trees.

Stubble-fields   black-ashen
with remorse — moldering
roots glittering with dream-
folded insects.

Levitating rains darken burial plains, leaving only a black-mirrored sheath of embered sleep.

Midnight rooms sunken
into blackened sylvan
melodies. Blind spiders
bring down sorrowful
ironbark from the stars.

Slender larvae carefully drip
down from our sleepwalking
eyes. In forests of fir and
pine cold geometries silently
decay.

Clouds of doubtful ravens
swoop down on blackened
granite. Convulsed by cold
premonitions, quiet brains
squabble over the debris of
forgotten forests.

Night. The weeds of
the elm and yew trees
silently close in over
us. They will never
again open.

Derision of earthly rot, beneath long-deserted anatomies, elder trees plaintively at work — pallid, dreamlike, dripping dark, swaying in monochromatic sorrow, fluttering upwards in black shale, encircling the stellar decay of our waxen fingers, submerged in blue-gray shivering, while shrouded clouds conspire over muted forests.

Rows of black pine in
their   sleep   murmur
melodies subterranean.

Under a canopy of nocturnal shale, our eyes gently dissipate in luminescent night — unstable, raven-limbed, drifting over still ponds of bristling charcoal, seething silence, impersonal night, growing down ruined walls, diamond-pure rains, promise of unfathomed abyss, gazing calmly at the whispering stillness of black stars.

Over cold prisms of mottled black
and brown, ash trees hover in
vesper-sung enclosures. Starlings
drift upwards from arborous night,
plunging into our skulls hollowed-
out, shimmering in diadem cataracts
that slowly billow in and out with
the tranquility of decay.

Across the black surface of ancestral planets, faint overtones of burnt tallow seep into ruinous bone. Brittle roots spiral upwards with obsidian precision. Slipping into darkness, trembling boughs secretly cultivate impossible anatomies.

Sullen, suspicious, mottled and overgrown — chaotic premonitions leak into our haloed dreams. Dispersed silence, shadowed, carbon-drenched, nocturnal without end. Cold splendors.

Frenetic anatomies cautiously emerge from hiding. A circle of black oak spreads outwards. Inverted stars.

Blackened skies of unreflective
shale. Rows of weather-beaten
winter pine drift across evening
in lattices of sorrow.

Luminous in their muted distance, trembling towers of burnt jade and obsidian. Sad and ashen, crows consumed in their contempt spin slowly towards a number unfathomed.

Bracken leaves reach suspicious in crimson
and mottled ash. The algebra of derision.
Gem-laden creatures drift menacing from
blackened camphor trees.

Cathedrals of cold cypress shimmer in the dazed silence of dusk. Furtive and gleaming rot arcs back towards distant melodies. Striations of hemlock and burnt oak whisper a vaporous logic into our weary, quicksilver husks.

Moss-ridden sparrows silently trace out manic sighs. Doubtful tendrils creep upwards, boring into the sinews of our coniferous bones. Deserted rooms, empty stars, gigantic slabs of concrete molded by deep time.

Roaming twilight of the larch trees erodes the dark augur of our most sacred invertebrates. From heavy eyes drips black dew. Inhuman shapes fearfully reach into our black myrtle remains.

Reflective blackshale cries a quiet calculus. Midnight plumes leak down luminous purple from incense pine. Impersonal gloom. Graphite-weighted limbs sink into blackened soil, entwined spiders and rotting wreaths. Heavy brains open gently onto darkened cryptids of contempt.

Night. Vast swaths of silk
trees form unhuman and
sepulchral shapes. Swarms of
night-rooks undulate outwards
into black stars. Festering
creatures attempt to decipher
distillate and scattered signs.

Black waters crawl towards our
naked feet. Backlit by night,
inverted geologies of blackened
purple pass slowly by. Imperfect
rows of katsura trees constellate
the horizon, dead in prayer.

Reeling blackwood acacia — nocturnal branches quietly outline our sleeping. Gloaming alder and ash weightlessly hover over lichen-fed limbs. Withered, diadem fatigue. Shadows. In the distance, the rustling of nameless things produces a nameless sorrow.

Skies of leaden slate hover noiselessly over axioms of grim attrition. Hushed air scintillates in its wraithlike stillness. Often, a tenebrous dread emerges in billows of moss and lichen. Blackened green.

Blighted forests drift above
us. Scattered remnants of
obsidian and purple flicker
across timidly-marked tombs.

Somber contours of winter fir
hang frenetically still. In distant
shadows of arborous dusk,
distant weeping of the unborn.
Algae in blacked green stray
quietly down corridors of stars.

Black oils seep from every pore.
From every sinew of every nerve and
tendon and bone the blackwood trees
emerge. Our limbs, rotting fusing —
fruiting epiphytes flower in luminous
shades of purple.

Vast lattices of black shale engulf us while we sleep. Primordial roots hunch over, as if in prayer. Arching acacia and star pine whisper spectral apprehensions. Black opal rains submerge everything permanent.

Under the scrawled effigy of night, plum trees quietly contort. Expanse of doubt that withers softly. Dexterities of lichen. Sullen growths. Jeweled black lavender arrays itself around furtive convulsions. Rotting purple floating precariously on hesitant superstitions.

Cavalcades of cedar and pine, encircling everything from above, tendrils pointing downwards to blackened earth. Clouds of jackdaws echo at random intervals. A quiet splashing in furrows moist in purple and black. Lavender fields, spindly and shivering. Nameless theorems bleeding out softly in the rising mists.

In black depths, shimmering creatures bow before death. Our crouched and sullen torsos, mottled with coniferous growths, illuminated in blacklights, the laments of dark orange and dirtied mauve. Emptied husks that meekly decay. Gem-filled articulations emerge from weightless black soil.

From forest temples of faded sorrow, something carefully smoulders. Cypress and black oak spill slowly across our starless sleep. Deciduous. Doleful. The darkened jade of the night sky seems to rotate.

Furtive rustling of
funeral brains, quietly
dispersed across star
pine and black tallow.
In the night, ashen
shapes sigh themselves
asleep.

Black sparrows twist around fading
harmonies. Wandering reeds drip
into the dense fog of sorrowful
wounds. The larch trees hover in a
numberless array.

Silk trees rise reeling before
our tired eyes. Blackoaks
loom in muted melodies.
Beneath our leprous fingers
moss and black shale
wavering impervious.

Gem-encrusted horns spin black-gray sorrows from the tallow trees. Star lichen cascade down sullen corridors. Dead eyes contemplate.

The nocturnal plumage of the katsura trees rustles in shades of violet, striated stretching along the luminous echoes of asylum symmetries.

Cold. Clear. From
the high circles of
star pine drifts a
melody of crystalline
lethargy.

Tendrils of black
opal gloaming in
shrill silence.

Forest of tombs.
Black rock, snow,
and burnt amber.

Creatures of oblivion,
submerged in black
pools. The larch trees
circle and wait.

Dreamless sleep
heavy as the hues
of the night forest.

Ominous ridges breathe in snow,
sunless forests breathe out mist.
Buried beneath dim weeds, the
willows grow dark, their wind-
borne tendrils suspended and
withering — owls drifting obscure
and unhallowed.

What forests do
you seek in the
vastness of sleep?

Stars float downwards into damp mud. Blackened jasper silently touches our fingers, turning them the color of shimmering ash.

Drawn on black threads of
amethyst and quartz. Our
shapeless sleep becomes
translucent, buried in night-
time prisms of moss. Glass
silhouettes.

Anagrams resembling
epitaphs, hung high in
tourmaline forests.

Plumes of bruised camphor
calmly dissipate in impersonal
night. Burial chambers of black
ink and heavy onyx.

Black depression sinks down.
Timidity.   The   soil-soaked
patience of crystalline roots.

Rotting fruit, black tears,
muted emerald night — the
charnel grounds of sentience,
sprouting dolorous limbs and
the slender sorrows of turgid
sleep.

Moss billowing below the stairs. Flash of night. Mouths engulf the darkness. Silkworms fan out across ocean floors. Forty thousand feet of black hair — our sorrow began long ago.

Charcoal-black night
murmuring among
birch trees. Hushed
lichen glow across
our skin.

A knot of spiders —
sulphur-split crows —
evergreen forests rise
whirling above us.

Moss-ridden limbs
drip thickly, glowing
amid vast arrays of
inconsolable aphids.

Rows of hovering incense
pine — slow shadows
peeling from blackened walls
— scattered, wraithlike,
starless quivering lassitude.

Staggering blackened and
leafless — sleeping gloom,
swirling decay, a flutter in
deserted cloisters.

The moss begins to glow —
anagrams of sorrow — cold
ravens — blackbirds and deer
— frost. Black ink. Dried nettle.

A sorrow above the
spheres, willows beneath
black ponds — graphite
arcs towards stars in our
heavy marrow.

Twilight and blackthorn wallows
in your hair — sleeping stillness
of burial trees held high in
ageless silk and tallow.

Incense scattered into blackened wounds. Leprous shapes dart furtively in our sleep. Silvered melancholy drifts upwards from star pine. Sleepless eyes black as coal. November's graphite decay.

Emaciated anatomies in
onyx and black shale
congeal in the shadows of
a green nocturne.

Ashen and leering, resignation
sinks nightly quiet into verdant
pools. Rustling beneath buried
sable skies.

In the reverie of gray
matter sleeping insects
glow obsidian and are
extinguished.

Vast epiphyte figures float upwards,
opening and closing all around us in
drowsy geometric sleep.

Winter night silently
drizzles downwards
from black forests.
Cold planets flicker
inside us.

Tendrils blighted with the
rot of cocoons — we
descend winding paths of
blackbriar   and   ancient
fern.

The ascent of moss and lichen. The descent of sleep.

On black altars of rotted oak
and fir — all premonitions
quietly tremble in sifting
dreamless sleep.

.

The greening sap of our
sullen limbs drips fearfully
into hovels of black onyx.

Precipitous vines cast adrift
in a lifeless tangle of obsidian
suspicion. Black sparrows in
amethyst quietly call.

Moss-covered glare of sleep, descending in a silent chasm. Wavering lianas gently graze on our temples.

The black patience
of what is ceaseless.

Tears distilled from labradorite envelop our entwined eroded limbs. Sleeping premonitions rustle and levitate. Quiet fluttering of night dislodges green veins. Ominous signs seep from our sullen anatomies.

Strange timbres of
lost forests drift over
the heavy tendrils of
our sleep.

In gilded books of forgotten
reason, withering ivy convulses
in black pain — frenzied
circling of locusts luminous in
the abyss of deduction and
reverie.

Viridescent larvae, furrowed and
forsaken — collapsing structures,
luminous latticework — sighs of
the unborn sinking under stars.

Slow erosion of sleep —
wandering mossy — cold
limbs headlong into night
— gardens of cloistered
oblivion — inanimate sleep
of long-dead species.

Forests that sigh — seething
doubts devolve along your
spine. In long hours of lead,
wings reach down in cold
lichen sleep.

Fleshless diadems — black
sustenance of despair.

Weightless withering of shapes
long forgotten — in forested
mausoleums, scholars of single
candles cultivate their epiphyte
contentment. Luminous planets
move more slowly than we can
see —

Inscrutable sparrows flutter over
the dark corners of the planet —
we have dedicated our dripping
flesh to the obscure contours of
this forest.

Wild lichen sink slower and lower
than our own crouched and sullen
listening. Arborous shapes scatter
from black skies — black spiders
in their tearless weeping — why
do I tell you these things? — you
are not even here.

All our diligent theorems
prisms of sleep — stretched
heavy in blackened emerald
blocks of luminous salt and
unraveling ferns.

Tenebrous crows silently recede into the blackened flurries of the brain. Wavering lianas hover in disarray. Blue limbs arc and billow. A quiet storm of spiders echoes tenuously towards divinity.

What dissipates
in black forest
night.

gnOme is a secret press specializing in the publication of anonymous, pseudepigraphical, and apocryphal works from the past, present, and future.

"Renounce the world, so that you may enjoy it." (*Chāndogyopaniṣad*)

gnOme is acephalic. All profits from print sales go to the authors.

gnomebooks.wordpress.com